PENWORTHAM, HUTTON & LONGTON IN FOCUS

Catherine Rees

2004
Landy Publishing

ISBN 1 872895 43 3

A catalogue record of this book is available from the British Library.

Layout by Sue Clarke   Tel: 01772 703751
Printed by Naylor the Printer Ltd., Accrington. Tel: 01254 234247

Landy Publishing have also published:

Accrington's Changing Face by Frank Watson & Bob Dobson
Accrington's Public Transport 1886-1986 by Robert Rush
A Blackburn Miscellany edited by Bob Dobson
Blackburn Tram Rides by Jim Halsall
Blackburn in Focus by Alan Duckworth & Jim Halsall
Bolland Forest & the Hodder Valley by Greenwood & Bolton
Bygone Bentham by Joseph Carr
A Century of Bentham by David Johnnson
Cockersand Abbey by Brian Marshall
Northward by Anthony Hewitson
Oswaldtwistle Observed by Mike Booth & Albert Wilkinson
Preston in Focus by Stephen Sartin
A Preston Mixture edited by Bob Dobson

A full list is available from:

Landy Publishing
'Acorns' 3 Staining Rise, Staining, Blackpool, FY3 0BU
Tel/Fax: 01253 895678

INTRODUCTION

This book came about some time ago through the purchase of a collection of local picture postcards from Mr Arthur Duffell of New Longton, a keen postcard collector with interest in local history who expressed the wish that his fine collection should be kept together rather than being sold piecemeal.

The postcards were brought to my notice and I was asked to compile a book around them. I was delighted to take on this challenge, and have thoroughly enjoyed researching for it. This research has been undertaken in libraries, country lanes, farmhouse kitchens, the odd 'pub and in Ernie Coxhead's comfy "shed". I have lived all my life in Penwortham, yet working on the book has taken me to places within easy reach that I have never previously come across. Listening to long-time residents of the villages has been both informative and pleasurable.

I have tried to create a journey for these pages. Starting in Lower Penwortham, we move through Whitestake to Higher Penwortham. Then onto Midge Hall, Hutton and Howick Cross, before arriving at New Longton (formerly known as Howick) and Longton.

For help received during my research, I want to thank the staff at the Lancashire Record Office and the Local Studies Library, Bow Lane, Preston, the Harris Reference Library, Preston and Chorley Reference Library. Amongst the individuals who have been most helpful and generous with their time I would also like to thank Mr & Mrs Arthur Duffell, Mr & Mrs Thomas Blackett, the Coxhead family at Whitestake, Barbara Sutton, Harold Aspden, Mr & Mrs Henry Hesketh, Mr & Mrs Duncan Hilton, Jackie Eccles, Betty Chadwick, Leslie Howarth, Jack & Dave Clarke, Mr & Mrs Frank Cookson, Peter Grant, Mr Scott the newsagent, Jane Riding Smyth, Gwen Smith and Colin Stansfield,. I especially thank Dick and Beryl Caunce who always made me welcome.

Last but by no means least, thank you to my husband Dave, nephew Joe Minniss and Annie O'Doherty for keeping me company on my travels.

Cath Rees

Catherine Rees
Penwortham, August 2004

Entrance to Penwortham Village, Preston.

Looking towards Lower Penwortham in the early 1900s. To the left is the road to the old bridge across the River Ribble. The bridge first opened in 1755, but after collapsing, it was rebuilt and opened in 1759. Tolls were charged on occasion to pay for its maintenance. Crossing Leyland Road is the West Lancashire Railway that ran from Southport to Preston until its closure in 1964.

THE CINDER PAD, PENWORTHAM.

2263.

The cinder pad running alongside the route of the old Southport railway line. It provided access from Cop Lane to the bridge over the river, and is today a pleasant track for cycling and walking. To the left is the Leyland Road Methodist Church, opened in about 1910, replacing the small Wesleyan Chapel on Pear Tree Brow.

Riverview Terrace, Riverside Road, built in 1889. The ferry across the Ribble had operated since before the 14th century, and as seen in this view, was still being used for pleasure trips until the early 1900s.

Two views of 'Old Boat House Row' which was at the far end of Riverside Road, next to the old boat house. The card (left) can be dated pre-1918, whilst the one below is postmarked 1937.

By 1938 the houses had been demolished, though the trunk of the tree on the left still stands today. The cottages were owned by Joshua Margerison of the White Windsor Soapworks in Preston. The 1901 census shows they were let to a shopkeeper, grocer's porter, cycle factor and a plumber.

Penwortham near Preston

This bungalow stood at the lower end of Valley Road. It was the lodge of The Oaks, the home of cotton manufacturer John Cooper. Near to the Oaks was Lower Farm, where Mr. Cooper gained experience as a gentleman farmer. This view photographed in the early 1900s, looks across the river towards Broadgate. At the time, the lodge was lived in by John Wilson, a gardener, who came from Westmorland.

By the 1890's, the Middleforth area along Leyland Road was being developed. Lyndale Terrace, built in 1899, between Dove Avenue and Lark Avenue, is typical of the terraced housing constructed. The photographer has gathered a group of children to pose outside the shop of fruiterer and market gardener J. Parker, whose assistant stands in the doorway.

Opposite Lyndale Terrace, semi-detached villas were built. Here, in about 1905, can be seen the canopied shop of grocer and provision dealer, Thomas Jackman, now the site of a motorcycle dealer.

MARGARET ST. PENWORTHAM.

By 1910, the houses on the west side of Margaret Road had been built. Building was still in progress when this scene was captured – the road itself still unlaid. Up until the 1930s, it was called Margaret Street. Talbot Road, in the same development area, was until the late 1930s, split into two sections, the stretch leading into Leyland Road being Eccles Street.

As Middleforth was being developed, concern was growing about the supply of mains water and the primitive sewage system. In 1898, Dr. Trimble, the Medical Officer of Health, reported that many property owners in the area refused to use the new mains supply preferring rainwater, rather than having to pay water rates. Sewage removal, or scavenging, was still carried out by men with a horse and cart well into the 1920s. Dr. Trimble referred to it as *"a public scandal"*. By 1928 he was at last able to announce the completion of the new sewers as *"a godsend"*. Road and path conditions fared little better. In 1911, Reverend Finch of Penwortham Hall complained about the *"positively dangerous"* state of Marshall's Brow, and recommended *"tar spraying or otherwise, the whole length from the bridge to Middleforth Brow."*

Middleforth is also known as Bunnock, and the people who live there are 'Bunnocks'. The term is usually meant to refer to someone who is simple minded, but locals will know the real meaning of the word! Story tells that a treacle wagon delivering to shops overturned at the top of Pear Tree Brow sending broken barrels rolling down the hill. Middleforth housewives rushed out to scoop up the treacle and used it to make bunnock, or parkin. The village men, most of who worked on the nearby railways, took the cake for their baggin'. Other labourers who had moved to the area to find work had not heard of parkin referred to as bunnock, and soon the name was applied to anyone who lived in Middleforth.

Recipe for bunnock cake.

8oz (225g) medium oatmeal	6oz (175g) sugar
4oz (100g) plain flour	8oz (225g) treacle
2tsp. ground ginger	½ tsp. bicarbonate of soda
4oz (100g) margarine	a little milk
1 egg	

Mix oatmeal, flour and ginger in a bowl. Melt margarine, sugar and treacle in a saucepan, and add dry ingredients. Mix bicarbonate of soda with a little milk, and add egg. Combine all ingredients, beating well. Spoon mixture into greased shallow baking tin. Bake in slow oven for about 1and ½ hours. Remove from oven and allow to cool in the tin. When cold, cut bunnock into squares.

Oven – 300deg. F/ 150deg. C. Gas Mark 2.

The Pear Tree Inn photographed in about 1910. Until the late 1840s it was a weaver's cottage. The arrival of steam powered mills in Lancashire forced the decline of handloom weaving and the cottage became a beer house. James Loxham, the landlord, is taking delivery of his beer barrels from the drayman. In 1913 James was complaining about his rent. In a letter to the inn's estate agents he writes that he has "*considerable less land than previous tenants*" and that the meadow next door "*is overrun by children and members of the cricket club*". To add insult to injury, he was forbidden to keep pigs and cattle, something previous landlords had been able to do. According to more recent licensees, James Loxham has been seen to be still keeping a watch on what's happening inside his old beer house. Just down from the inn can be seen the old Wesleyan Methodist Chapel which opened in 1819. Now in use as a garage, the chapel was closed when the new Methodist Church next to the Bridge Inn was built.

Before being called Leyland Road, this stretch of the Preston-Wigan turnpike was known as Penwortham Lane, a name that is still in use for the general area. On the left is the Sumpter Horse Inn, an old coaching inn – a sumpter being a packhorse. To the right are the gardens of Railway Terrace, three cottages that were owned by the London and North Western Railway Company, and let to railway workers. The photographer has caught the attention of some little girls, but what is the toddler on the other side of the road up to?

The Black Bull Inn on Pope Lane appears on the 1840 tithe map of Penwortham as a brewery, with a smithy next door. When this photograph was taken in the early 1900s, Thomas Riley and his wife Alice were the innkeepers. The area was then quite rural and undeveloped. The row of cottages to the left were known by the original owner's name – Brown's Row, and were first let out to handloom weavers who worked at home.

POPE LANE, PENWORTHAM.

In 1901, the cottages were lived in by seven families with the wage earners variously employed as farm labourers, an under gamekeeper, a blacksmith and a brewer. Whilst exploring Penwortham, local historian Anthony Hewitson described in 1911 how the cottages used to have " *a rather depressing, forlorn appearance…. now they are apparently all in good order…. a spirit of finery has got amongst them*". Long since demolished, the site of Roger Brown's cottages is now occupied by the Co-op and other retail premises.

Thatched cottages on the stretch of Pope Lane that used to be called Workhouse Lane. The row of cottages above was situated to the left of the old workhouse, and the single storey cottage below was opposite Lindle Lane. People living here would have their own smallholdings or be employed on one of the larger farms in and around Whitestake. William Bamford, who lived in the house below, was a cowman employed on the Lancashire County Council farm. The rich, fertile land of the moss around this area is still home to many agricultural businesses.

One of the few listed buildings in the Penwortham-Whitestake area is Nutters Platt Farm on the corner of Lindle Lane. The date stone above the door tells us that the house was built in 1653 by William Mawdesley. When this photograph was taken in the early 1900s it was occupied by farmer Henry Knowles and his family. A platt was a small wooden or stone bridge that crossed the waterways of the moss. Nutters Platt crossed Mill Brook.

Cop Lane Halt on the Southport-Preston line in 1936. It was the only station in Penwortham, opened in 1911. This view is looking towards Preston, the first bridge being Cop Lane, with Cromwell Road off to the left. In 1964 the line was closed, and the cutting is now in use as the route of the Penwortham bypass.

Broad Oak Lane was originally called Back Lane. It was a track across the moss until the land was gradually reclaimed and improved. Smallholdings began to appear like the one shown here on the corner with Cop Lane. On the 1840 tithe map it is listed as Plot 418, occupied by James Miller.

Cop Lane viewed from outside the water tower. Just behind the lady and girls is the entrance to Rawstorne Road, which used to be called Penwortham Hill until housing development began around 1910. Even at the end of the 1920s Cop Lane was still very rural, the road was unmade with a ditch running down each side. The few cottages that existed were the old crofts, or farms, which were surrounded by open fields.

Thatched cottages on Cop Lane, standing near to where the Girls' Grammar School is today. The two boys, in their Sunday best, pose with a hoop.

Photographed in about 1940, Liverpool Road was developing into the shopping area we know today. Looking across from the corner of Priory Lane can be seen the Midland Bank, Mrs. Sutton's outfitters shop, hairdresser Mrs. Edmunds, confectioner Mr. Webster, Mrs. Hodgson's gown shop, Mr. Desmond the newsagent, and T.L. Robinson Ltd, wine merchants.

The week of July 6th 1913 witnessed an historic royal occasion when King George V and Queen Mary visited Lancashire. Penwortham celebrated the visit with a British Empire pageant held in the grounds of the Priory. The King and Queen passed through Penwortham on the 8th of July, welcomed by huge crowds along the route of Liverpool Road, down to Broadgate and into Preston. The procession assembled on Priory Lane, seen here with the old Sunday school in the background, before taking their places on the hill to cheer the royal party. Afterwards, the pageant was performed at the Priory with Miss Livesey as Britannia and Miss Elsie Rawkins as England. The Preston Guardian reported: *at the close of the pageant.... the National Anthem was fervently sung, and with a special significance in view of the day's events*".

NEXT WEEK'S ROYAL VISIT
TO LANCASHIRE.

OFFICIAL TIME TABLE OF THE TOUR.

WHERE TO SEE THEIR MAJESTIES.

FAST.—Along Liverpool-road, through Bellow and Tarleton.
SLOW.—At Bank Hall.
FAST.—To Much Hoole.
SLOW.—From St. Michael's Church, Hoole, to Rose and Crown.
FAST.—From Cookson Row to Raikes Row.
FAST.—Along road to Walmer Bridge.
SLOW.—Police Station to Nelson-terrace.
FAST.—To Longton.

SLOW.—Between Windmill House and Police Station (children between the school and church).
FAST.—To Penwortham.
SLOW.—Down the hill (children massed for pageant).
FAST.—Thence into Preston to foot of Fishergate-hill, except that there may be a slackening along Broadgate.
SLOW.—Up Fishergate-hill and along Fishergate.
1 45—STOP.—Arrive Preston Town Hall for presentations in Market-square.
2 0—Lunch at the Bull and Royal Hotel.
3 0—SLOW.—Church-street and Stanley-street.
3 5—STOP.—Inspection of Messrs. Horrockses, Crewdson, and Co.'s Mill.
SLOW.—Along Stanley-street, Deepdale-road, Moor Park-avenue (school children on each side), Garstang-road, Moor-lane, Fylde-street, Fylde-road, Water-lane, and Tulketh-road.
FAST.—St. Michael's Church through Ashton.
SLOW.—Plough Hotel (children of Lea and Cottam).

Penwortham Church Lodge.

Penwortham Priory was the home of the Rawstorne family until about 1815 when they began to spend most of their time at Hutton Hall. The Priory was then leased to various tenants until it was demolished in 1925. Above can be seen the Priory lodge. When work on the new Penwortham Bridge began in 1912, the lodge was carefully dismantled and rebuilt on tolsey Drive, Hutton. Could the two young ladies be sisters Susannah and Ellen Sutton who lived in the lodge in 1901?

The bottom of Church Avenue at its junction with Penwortham Hill. Here stood Penwortham Priory Lodge until its removal when the road to Preston was widened in anticipation of increased traffic when the new bridge across the Ribble was built. This view in the early 1920s reveals little change in traffic flow.

Work in progress on Shaftesbury Avenue, Penwortham. By the start of the First World War, the Priory estate was gradually being sold to developers. After the war, what remained of the land was sold to Arthur Spencer, a local builder, who quickly transformed the area into what we know as Shaftesbury Avenue and Kensington Avenue. This view looks towards Priory Lane before it was extended to the north.

3229. HILL ROAD, PENWORTHAM

Hurst Grange Lodge on Hill Road. Early one morning in March 1900, the occupant, William Ravenscroft, coachman to John Forshaw of Hurst Grange, was surprised to find a baby abandoned on his doorstep. A note with the child read: *"keep this little baby for a few weeks. You will receive 5s. per week....cherish it as your own"*. The Preston Guardian, reporting the case, told of the mother's trial and how the case was dismissed when the chairman decided that the woman had meant no criminal intentions. She had left the child warmly wrapped, with clothes and money – *"I did not leave the child to be neglected. You will find that in the note"*.

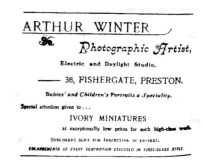

Penwortham Hill, Preston.

Photographed in about 1923, this shows a very quiet Penwortham Hill with transport old and new. The inscription on the cenotaph reads " *this tribute to the valour and sacrifice of our men whose names are here recorded was erected by the people of this parish A.D. 1920*". Most of the Penwortham men who lost their lives in the First World War served with the Loyal North Lancashire Regiment.

Work on the new Penwortham bridge began in 1912, and it was officially opened in June 1915. This view from the bottom of Fishergate Hill across the bridge shows a strangely empty road compared with today's flow of traffic. The bridge made access to Higher Penwortham much easier than the old route of travelling down Broadgate in order to cross the Ribble via the old 18th century bridge.

New Council Bridge, Preston.

23

Heath House on Sod Hall Lane, Midge Hall. The house was also known as Sod Hall, causing some confusion as there was an older building in the area also called Sod Hall. The earlier hall had eventually collapsed as it sank into the moss. Heath House was to suffer the same fate. By the 1940s it was splitting in two, and only one half was inhabitable even though there was no running water or electricity and the floor was sloping. In its heyday it had been a magnificent house with vast rooms and big windows overlooking the moss. There are accounts of a racetrack in the grounds where four-in-hand racing was held, and also mention of hare coursing events.

Pleasant View, Long Moss Lane in the late 1920s. Gathered outside is the Chorley Workers' Educational Association Rambling Club, as it was originally called. Rather well dressed on this occasion, the group had been on an educational ramble around the moss to learn about the agricultural businesses and the great variety of produce grown locally for the markets. Would Pleasant View have served refreshments for the visitors?

Sadly, no longer standing, this is the Round House which was on Sod Hall Lane. It had originally been a tollhouse where people had to pay 1d per wheel to cross the moss on their way to Leyland. The house had two rooms and a central hearth that burned peat dug from the moss. It was occupied by Wilfred Halliwell until June 1983 when it was hit by lightning and subsequently demolished. Mr. Halliwell had lived in the house with his parents from 1920 when he was 10 years old. Prior to the Halliwells moving into the Round House, Mrs. Warton was in charge of the tollgate. Could this be her on the postcard, which is dated pre-1918?

Saunders Lane viewed from the Chapel Lane end – a peaceful retreat before the intrusion of the Longton bypass. Just behind the disappearing right hand curve in the lane was Stephenson's Farm (below). The farm was owned by Lawrence Rawstorne who let it to John Stephenson.

Mayor's Farm, built in 1690 for Robert Mayor. A listed building, it is now known as Hutton Manor and stands in Moor Lane, Hutton.

26

In 1894, Lancashire County Council took over Lawrence Rawstorne's farm at Hutton. The estate was well equipped with buildings including a farmhouse, dairy, barns, cattle pens and poultry houses. The Gables, above, was the men's hostel until it became home to the farm manager and his family in 1924. Below is the milking parlour with the chimneys of the girls' hostel visible behind. Attempts were made to segregate the boys from the girls without much success it seems – sending a postcard to Billy in 1908, one young dairymaid wrote: "*in remembrance of happy times in the shippons*"!

HACKNEY STALLION,
PENWORTHAM SPORT,
Foaled 1913.
Sire—Royal Success (8,995).
Dam—(19,255) Lady Cass.
FEE, £2 2s. Groom's Fee, 2s. 6d.
PENWORTHAM SPORT is a whole coloured Chestnut; an extraordinary fine goer, bending knees and hocks, with any amount of dash and fire, in fact a perfect pony. He goes in harness with best of manners. His sire, Royal Success, is the sire of all the best harness ponies of the day. His splendid breeding is bound to ensure his success at stud.
All Mares at Owner's risk.

Owner: A. R. FISH.
HOLME MEAD, HUTTON, Nr. PRESTON.

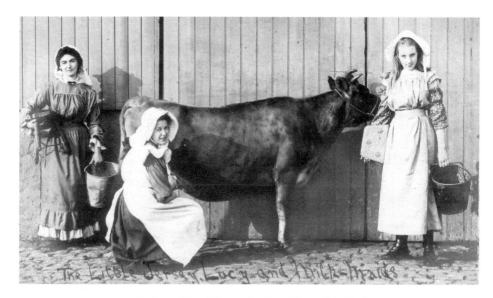

Dairymaids at the agricultural farm, Lindle Lane.

Students at the college were aged 15 and over. Their board and lodging was free provided they stayed for at least eight weeks. There were courses in agriculture, poultry keeping, fruit and vegetable preservation and bacon curing. The main activity was dairy farming. Cheese and butter was sold across the country, including several varieties of French cheeses, which of course under modern EEC rulings would be forbidden. One of the best selling cheeses of the farm was Lancashire cream slice described as being *very attractive with salads* and *a lucrative method of dealing with unsold milk*. Other courses were not so successful – experiments in growing oats were *spoiled by depredations of small birds*. Between 1939-1943, hundreds of women trained at the farm for the Women's Land Army. They came from all over the North West and as far afield as London and Northumberland.

Lancashire County Council Farm, Feb. 1906.

Hutton Hall had been in the possession of the Rawstorne family since the 17th century, but it was not until about 1815 that Lawrence Rawstorne decided to vacate Penwortham Priory, which was becoming an expensive burden, and make the hall his main residence. Hutton Hall remained with the family until the 1930s when it was put up for sale and purchased by Lancashire County Council. It became part of the newly formed Lancashire police headquarters, but was eventually demolished in 1961 to make way for further development of the site. All that remains of the hall are the gateposts, standing opposite Moor Lane, in line with the Rawstorne's old lodge removed from Penwortham.

The original Blue Anchor dates back to the mid 1700s when it was a welcome calling place for stagecoaches on the road from Liverpool to Preston. By the turn of the century Liverpool Road was a major trunk road and in the 1920s work began on building the Anchor Inn we know today. During the Second World War it was a popular venue for dance bands, and post war saw large numbers of coach parties visiting on their way to the Blackpool illuminations.

• The Lounge. •

ANCHOR INN, HUTTON, NR PRESTON.

Pre.37

Hutton Post Office in about 1915. It was situated on Liverpool Road opposite Hutton Grammar School. Next door to the post office was a tuck shop, a regular haunt of the grammar school boys, as it sold pies and confectionery.

Cockerton Farm on the corner of Skip Lane and Grange Lane, Hutton. It is little changed today. Below is Joseph Swindlehurst of Cockerton Farm, who also delivered coal around the area.

J. F. Swindlehurst,
COAL MERCHANT,
Longton Bridge Station.

Residence : Cockerton Farm,
Skip Lane, Hutton.
All orders promptly attended to.

Hutton Grammar School in 1911, with the headmaster Rev. Thomas Cunningham, his wife and members of staff. The Charity Commissioners praised Mr. Cunningham – *"the headmaster.... has been most successful and deserves every encouragement"*. Below – The headmaster's house, no longer in use, but awaiting refurbishment.

The history of Hutton Grammar School begins in 1552 when Christopher Walton founded a charity school in Longton. The children were to be taught *"absay, catechism, primer, accidence, perverly"*, [sic] and education was free to the children of Penwortham parish. By the 1740s it was decided that Longton was inconvenient for most children to attend school, so land was bought in Hutton and the grammar school was born. The 1901 Charity Commissioners' report states that there were 78 boys in the school, 48 of them boarders. Most of the boys were local, but others came from as far afield as Manchester, Barrow and Carlisle.

The Gates of Honour at the front of the school. The inscription reads
"Hold in Honour all ye who enter here those old Huttonians who went forth to served in the Great War 1914-1919".

Part of the old school photographed (right) in about 1907. The building to the left has been altered and the little porch has disappeared, but the building on the right looks much the same today.

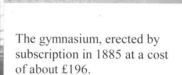

The gymnasium, erected by subscription in 1885 at a cost of about £196.

The school rugby XV 1925-26.

In 1727 a charity school had been founded at Howick Cross. By 1880 the present school had been built at a cost of £1,888 6s 4d. In 1899 the attendance at the school was 55 pupils. This photograph shows the pupils practising their drill exercises. Mrs. Eleanor Greenwood was headmistress in around 1913.

Farm labourers at Old Grange Farm, Grange Lane, Hutton. The farm had originally belonged to the monks of Penwortham Priory and then passed to the Rawstorne family when they bought the Priory. In 1915 Squire Rawstorne sold the farm to Captain Waring who managed it until Lancashire County Council bought the Hutton and Howick estate as part of their post war smallholdings scheme to provide plots of land for ex-servicemen to farm. Old Grange was unsuitable for being split up into small units and was bought by the Hon. Lord Vestey in 1922. During the 1930s the Hesketh family were tenants at the farm but eventually were able to buy it in 1946/47, and still live there today.

Haystacking in the stackyard, Old Grange Farm. It was all hands on deck at hay time, and to haul the hay up to make the huge stacks a tall grab pole was used, as seen in this picture.

Henry Hesketh, standing on the right with his farmhands who helped during hay time. Standing first left is Archibald Tattersall, third from the right is Henry Blake and kneeling second right is Harry Swindlehurst.

Old Grange Farm: the ladies in the photographs had come to help Henry Hesketh's wife Catherine with the cheese making.

The history of All Saints Church, New Longton begins in October 1866 when the first Sunday service was held in a cottage on Station Road. A schoolroom was also set up there. By July 1867 the new chapel school had been built, being used as a school during the week and holding services on Sundays.

Miss Mary Jardine was appointed as headmistress of the school in 1882 and remained there for 37 years. She was a leading light in village life. On the right is the Sunday school, photographed in 1914.

As the parish grew, fund raising began to build a new church at a cost of £1,100. The wooden church, (right), was built in 1921 and dedicated in January 1922. The old chapel school was extended and has been the village school ever since. The wooden church served the parish until 1964 when the present All Saints Church on Station Road was opened. The wooden building was dismantled and re-erected in Tarleton, where it is part of Websters' furniture showrooms.

Prior to the railway station opening in New Longton in 1899, the village, then known as Howick, was very small with just a few scattered dwellings. The railway enabled people to commute to work in Preston, and from the late 1890s onwards, Station Road and Chapel Lane were soon filled with large villas built for the wealthy industrialists who wanted to escape from town life. Above can be seen houses standing opposite All Saints Church. 'Hill View', the detached house in the middle was built in 1902. The photograph below shows the row of houses on Chapel Lane next to the playground. The villa nearest is dated 1898.

Photographed in about 1920, these houses still look much the same today, though the large telegraph pole has since been replaced with one of smaller proportions. Off to the right is South Avenue.

Houses on Chapel Lane opposite the post office and Methodist Church. Heane's stationery and printing company of Preston produced most of these picture postcards of New Longton.

Looking towards Station Road from approximately Park Avenue. A modern house now stands to the left of the semi-detached houses. The picture below shows the same row of houses from the opposite direction. Deliverymen with horses and carts still called selling produce well into the 1930s and 40s.

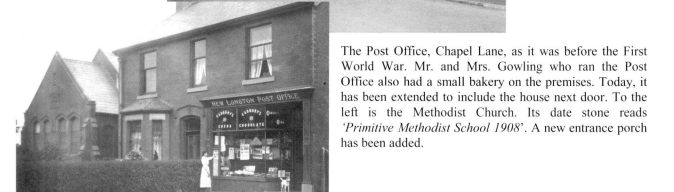

The Post Office, Chapel Lane, as it was before the First World War. Mr. and Mrs. Gowling who ran the Post Office also had a small bakery on the premises. Today, it has been extended to include the house next door. To the left is the Methodist Church. Its date stone reads *'Primitive Methodist School 1908'*. A new entrance porch has been added.

Two views of New Longton railway station, formerly known as Hutton and Howick railway station. Royalty Lane is to the right. The cottage in the foreground, seen in about 1910 with a thatched roof and (below) in the late 1920s with a tin roof, has been replaced by the newsagents, but the cottage to the right, with the porch still looks much the same today.

Above, the railway crossing on Station Road photographed after the Second World war from where the chemist's shop is today. The Cedars now occupies the site of the signal box, but the station office to the left has been little changed. The station is remembered as being very pretty with prize winning floral displays.

A wintry view from behind the signal box and station at New Longton. The station was well used by local businesses as well as passengers. Coal was delivered from Wigan and bagged at the sidings before being delivered throughout the village. Nurserymen sent out their produce from the station, and parcels arrived which were delivered to their destinations by the junior porter on his bike.

Gilbert Taylor, coal and coke merchant, with his horse and cart. He ran his delivery service from Hutton and Howick goods yard. Behind him can be seen the colliery wagons which brought the coal from the Wigan coalfields. This photograph was taken in about 1905.

Haydn Howard was a sign writer and coach painter. He worked at Hutton and Howick station in premises rented from Eric Sutcliffe. Here Haydn stands beside a recently finished wagon with its trade plates. One of the headlamps is covered showing that the photograph was taken during the Second World War. Haydn had his own musical band – Howard's Melody Boys.

43

Dawson's Farm, Chapel Lane, had belonged to the Wilson family from as early as the 1880s. Standing outside are Richard Wilson (2nd left) and his sons Dick and Will (3rd and 4th left). In the gateway is their brother Arthur. Twice a day milk was delivered to the neighbourhood by horse and cart, usually by the farmer's children before and after they went to school. The milk was poured from tubs, or kits, straight into the housewife's jug. Next to the outhouses is the hay cart. Though the farm buildings have all disappeared, the house itself has not changed much.

Pictured in the late 1940s is Bob Mawdsley with a cartload of potatoes. He grew up at Moorside Villa on Drumacre Lane with his father who was a poultry farmer. The Mawdsleys moved into the house in about 1906. It is uncertain who the ladies are standing outside the house, but according to the 1901 census returns they could be Mary, Elizabeth and Catherine Carr, daughters of Thomas Carr, with his granddaughter Margaret standing at the gate. The modern day Moorside Villa has undergone a complete transformation.

The earliest school in Longton was situated on Marsh Lane, but in 1818 the new chapel school was opened on Liverpool Road where the church hall now stands. In 1887 James Heald was appointed headmaster. The school log books give accounts of the pupils' progress but also report how village life was of great importance. Attendance at school was always very poor during haymaking, potato planting, harvesting and fruit picking as the children were needed at home on the farm. Epidemics of scarlet fever, mumps, whooping cough and other infections often closed the school for weeks on end. Drill took place weekly under the guidance of Major John Yeo from Fulwood Barracks. In 1908 Mr Heald writes *"increasing traffic is proving very disconcerting to schoolwork…besides being a real danger to the children when assembling or dismissing"*. Eventually, after nearly 37 years as headmaster, Mr. Heald resigned in 1923, due to the strain imposed by *"the passing traffic at almost all hours of the day"*.

Mr. Heald, the headmaster, with his pupils.

45

A treat for the children on July 8th 1913, when the school closed for the day so that they could cheer King George V and Queen Mary as they passed through the village. Here the pupils are gathered with St. Oswald's School before spending an afternoon in Mr. Swindell's field playing games.

December 23rd 1923, the final entry in the logbook reads *"this building ceases to be used as a Public Elementary School. On Monday January 11th the scholars will assemble for the first time in the New Longton Council School, which has been erected in School Lane"*. As the number of children increased, the Council School, seen on the right, would eventually become overcrowded and in the 1960s the present school was built. The new millennium would see the earlier School Lane building demolished to make way for new houses.

In 1807 the first Wesleyan Chapel was built on Marsh Lane, and then replaced in 1833. The present day chapel was built in 1872 and the earlier building was used as a school, until the new school opened on Liverpool Road.

The Primitive Methodist Chapel on Chapel Lane was built in 1837. Here, Mr. Heald the school headmaster stands outside. The congregation dwindled as it moved to the Marsh Lane and New Longton chapels, and now the building is unrecognizable having been converted into two houses, numbers 57 and 59 Chapel Lane.

St. Oswalds   Catholic Church

As the Catholic population of the Longton area grew, Father Cosgrave of St. Augustine's Church Preston looked for land to build a Catholic Church. With funds provided by the Dean of Chorley, the Church of St. Oswald's was built and opened in October 1894. It was to include a school for 60 children, a chapel and a teacher's house. A moveable screen was to separate the classroom from the chapel area. Mr. Maguire was the first teacher, and Father Myerscough the first parish priest. In 1896 Miss Wilson took charge of lessons and stayed until her retirement in 1919. In 1931 a new school was opened and the old chapel school was altered to become a place of worship. The church that stands today was opened in 1965 and the old building was adapted to become the social centre.

St. Andrew's Church seen on the left in about 1915 and below in about 1925. There has been a chapel on or near the site since the 12th century. An earlier church built in 1770 stood to the north of the present church which was completed in 1887. The bell and font are from the old church. The porch was added in 1892 and was supposed to carry a steeple, but it was never built.

The old vicarage, 'Glebe House', on the corner of Shirley Lane. It still looks the same today but is hidden behind tall hedges and fencing.

Longton Guides photographed in about 1936 with the vicar of St. Andrew's Church, the Reverend Girton.

St. Andrew's Band. 2nd from the right on the front row is Mr. Burrows. 4th from the right on the second row (if we include the drummer) is trombonist Ted Coxhead and 3rd from the left on the third row is Tom Rennie.

Photographed in about 1909, Longton stocks can be seen in front of the white house on the right. After removal, they spent some time as gate posts to a cottage on Franklands Fold, but are now situated outside the library. Further down, outside Kitty's Cottage, road works are in operation watched by a group of children. The old barn is now Longton Village Garage, and standing to its left is Kitty's Farm.

Looking towards the Ram's Head in about 1907 when T.H. Carter was the licensee. The cottages on the left have been demolished and in their place stand the post office, chemist and Spar shop.

With the Ram's Head on the left, Taylor's shop can be seen on the corner of School Lane. The billboards are reporting the Boer war, dating the photographs to about 1900. The same view, (below right) shows the shop when it had become Booths' first store in Longton, opening in 1927. The site is now occupied by other business premises.

The Ram's Head in the early 1900s. The notice beside the right window reads *'Southport Cycling Club Headquarters'*, while the projecting sign to the left advertises billiards and stabling.

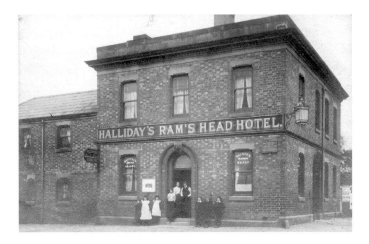

51

Café Monica, opposite the Ram's Head. Also known as "*Old Shep's*", it was a gathering place where the village youngsters could sit by the fire in the evening talking, playing cards and drinking pop provided by the owner Mr. Shepherd.

Before the vicarage on Shirley Lane became the home to the minister of St. Andrew's Church, this was the parsonage. By the 1920s it was home to the Gaskell family, plumbers and decorators, and also Longton's first fire service. To the right of the Old Parsonage was the Manor house, home to wealthy landowner Squire Breakell-Moss. The Old Parsonage is still there, but the Manor house has gone to be replaced by the New Manor home for the elderly.

By the 1930s Longton was well provided with leisure and sporting clubs such as football, hockey, folk dancing and as seen on the right, the bowls team.

Longton Stocks Football Club over the seasons. The earliest team photograph (1911-12) shows the players in trousers, whilst in the later pictures they are wearing shorts.

August 1919 saw Longton celebrate peace after the First World War. A full day of events was organised with a procession through the village ending in Marsh Lane where sports and tea were provided firstly for the children, and then later for the adults. A competition for the best decorated wagon saw 17 entrants, with R. Wright taking first prize. J. Dawson took second and T.R. Wilkins third.

Longton Bridge Station on the Southport-Preston line, seen in about 1909, and below in the 1950s. The station had platforms on both sides of the double track, and a large goods yard and sidings. It was a busy passenger and commercial centre until its closure in 1964. Local businesses used the station to send and receive goods. Coal arrived for the local merchants, and barley was delivered for Wilkins' Brewery. Next to the station were the brickworks, whose tall kiln chimneys can be seen. Thomas Ward started the brickworks in 1897, and from the 1950s until closing in the 60s when the clay pits had been exhausted, the Bentley Brickworks Company managed the site.

During the Second World War before the Home Guard was officially formed, Longton had its Local Defence Volunteers, referred to by the villagers as 'Look, Duck and Vanish' as the only equipment they had were sticks. They were soon transformed into the uniformed Home Guard, equipped with rifles. The Air Raid Precaution post, seen here, was situated on Back Lane, and there was also a lookout post at the Dolphin Inn where watch was kept over the marsh.

(Right) taken in about 1904 from near the Black Bull, this photograph shows a peaceful Liverpool Road. The policeman must have had a quiet day at work.

Two views of the Black Bull, the first in about 1920, the second ten years later. The inn was a coaching house, and at one time there had been a mortuary in a wooden hut next door. The earlier picture shows a tranquil scene of a farmer herding his cows down the road, while the later picture shows a taste of things to come with the arrival of the motorcar. The barn has been replaced with a car park, but Rose Cottage, to the right, is still there.

LONGTON VILLAGE. WRIGHT. PH

Four views of Ashleigh Terrace with the Red Lion Hotel on the left. They were photographed between 1910 and 1920. Today there is still a newsagent where John I'Anson kept his shop, but now on one side is an off licence and on the other is a solicitor's office.

Liverpool Road, Longton.

Liverpool Road, Longton.

RED LION
-HOTEL-

GARAGE

A closer view of Ashleigh Terrace shows the post office on the right, which also sold haberdashery, including knitting wool, thread and silks, and underwear! Next door was the local bank which opened between 10am and 2pm on Tuesdays and Fridays. The house next to the bank was the home of the National Telephone Company, with the switchboard in the front parlour. The houses to the left were the Oddfellows' Cottages before being turned into shops.

The Red Lion Hotel in the 1920s. There were stables at the rear, and the hotel was also used as an auction house. The door on the left has since been blocked up and the window to its top right still remains bricked in today. The sign shows the hotel to have been a meeting place for The Royal Antediluvian Order of Buffaloes.

Standing at what is now the corner of Grove Avenue, Ashleigh Terrace can be seen to the right. The two buildings to the left of the terrace were part of Home Farm that belonged to Mr. Wilkins of the brewery, who lived at The Grove. On the site of the farm now are retail premises and the Beeches Medical Centre.

In 1910 Richard Law was the landlord of the Golden Ball on the corner of Marsh Lane. During his tenancy the inn was the area headquarters of the Automobile Association. The Golden Ball was always a resting place for people travelling to Preston. There were stables and a coachman to look after the horses, while those on their way to market could tuck into a hearty breakfast. In the 1930s when Mrs. Nicholson was the landlady, high teas were provided for travellers

Posted in 1906, the card above is looking towards the junction of Marsh Lane with the Golden Ball on the left hand side. The cottage on the left was lived in by Polly Wilson who, according to the sender of the card, can be seen crossing the road.

Another view along Liverpool Road towards Marsh Lane corner. The white cottage in the distance is Bury's Cottage. The nearer house on the right side of the road was home and workplace to William Sutton, or "*Tailor Bill*" as he was known.

Above, looking towards the Golden Ball from Liverpool Road. The house on the right belonged to William Sutton. The photograph below shows the shop in more detail. William Sutton's father was also a tailor. Behind the shop was the little cottage workroom where Tailor Bill made all his suits; the cottage can still be seen today. Suttons were high class tailors; all the suits were handmade, and Longton villagers said they lasted a lifetime. The building is still there, opposite Birkdale Avenue. It is now a private residence and bares little resemblance to how it once looked, but it is still fondly known as Tailor Bill's. The postcard below was sent by William Sutton to his aunt and uncle, Mr. and Mrs. Waring.

Robinson's Garage, seen here in the late 1920s stood where H.B. Panelcraft is now situated. Its position on the Liverpool-Preston road would have ensured good business with the increasing numbers of motorised vehicles. The garage advertises its services which, apart from the sale of petrol and oil, included repairs and spare parts. The owner also provided a saloon car for private hire. To the left of the forecourt is an eye catching garden with the words *'petrol & oils'* cut into the grass verge. Another service, as the board on the telegraph pole announces, is a public telephone, useful in the days when not many people had their own 'phone at home.

The Grove   *Longton*

The Wilkins family had been brewing beer in Longton since the 1830s, and by the 1880s the business was thriving as one of the village's main employers. Richard and Mary Wilkins and their son Thomas lived very comfortably at The Grove, seen here c. 1900. Besides employing many villagers at their Marsh Lane brewery, others worked at The Grove as servants, cooks and gardeners. The Wilkins also owned much of the farming land in Longton that was let to tenant farmers. Mr. Wilkins travelled about the village in a horse drawn carriage. After the death of Thomas Wilkins The Grove was sold in the late 1920s and the family lived at Plumpton House, next to the brewery. During the Second World War The Grove was a base for the Royal Army Service Corps. After several years as a repair depot for the lawnmower manufacturer Atco, The Grove was demolished to make way for new housing. All that remains of this once splendid house are the gates and driveway.

Longton had its windmill. The villagers and farmers from around would take their grain to the mill for grinding. Longton mill was situated on Liverpool Road opposite the entrance to Birkdale Avenue. When this photograph was taken in the early 1900s the mill had long since lost its sails.

Mr. And Mrs. Duckworth chose this view of their house, Old Mill Cottage, to send Christmas greetings in the early 1900s. James Banister and his family moved into the cottage in about 1919 having previously lived at Park Farm on Marsh Lane. Old Mill Cottage, situated towards the Marsh Lane end of Liverpool Road is now not as open to view at it was when this photograph was taken.

MAY PEACE, GOODWILL, & PROSPERITY BE YOURS THIS HAPPY CHRISTMASTIDE. From Mr & Mrs Duckworth. Old Mill Cottage Longton.

Park Farm (it was also known as The Parks) at the corner of Park Farm Close on Marsh Lane was home to James Banister, his wife and daughters when this photograph was taken in 1905. Mr. Banister was a hay and straw dealer and a coal merchant. Here the family can be seen in the garden. The Parks was built in 1750.

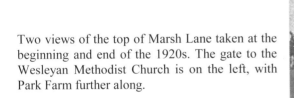

Two views of the top of Marsh Lane taken at the beginning and end of the 1920s. The gate to the Wesleyan Methodist Church is on the left, with Park Farm further along.

Many years ago the houses along Marsh Lane would have looked much the same as the one pictured on the right. There was no running water, gas or electricity and this situation didn't begin to change much until the 1930s. Just before the Second World War most of the old thatched cottages were demolished in a familiar scene of modernisation by local councils

Moss's Farm, Marsh Lane. Standing outside the farm in about 1926 is Mrs. Margaret Wright. The buildings were demolished in the early 1990s to make way for a nursing and residential home.

Looking towards the top of Marsh Lane, the Old Farmhouse is the first cottage on the right with Lily Cottage next to it.

This is Taylor's Farm, Marsh Lane, home to the Chew family from 1928-1952. The house had been built around a much older cottage. In springtime the garden made an eye catching sight with its hundreds of snowdrops. The gentleman could be Mr. Wright who owned the farm before he sold it to Mr. Chew. The house was knocked down in the mid '50s and a bungalow now stands on the site.

Blackhurst Farm was home to Nicholas Wright and his family before they moved to Ellerslie Farm. Blackhurst Farm has seen its changes, though the decorative door arch remains. Longton Swimming Pool is now situated here.

Norris House, Marsh Lane, was home to Herbert and Catherine Dandy and their family.

Sea View was built in the 1880s, and like many of the old houses down Marsh Lane it has seen repairs and alterations over the years. In 1901 William and Elizabeth Harrison and their five children lived at one side, and George and Letitia Strickson and their three daughters lived in the other half. As the Strickson girls grew up they would be known throughout the village as *'Faith, Hope and Charity'* because of their involvement with St. Andrew's Church.

Here is Rose Farm in the early 1900s when it was home to the Hindles. It still stands today opposite the end of Back Lane

Mr. Heathcote (right) lived in a cottage beyond the *"Flying Fish"* (The Dolphin Inn) next to the marsh. Here he stands at his door proudly showing the wild geese he has just bagged.

George Wright of Ellerslie Farm, Hall Carr Lane, with a group, including his brothers on Longton Marsh.

69

A young Hugh Harrison stands with his parents outside his home, Marsh Farm, Back Lane, Longton. Taken in about 1910, the photograph shows how the farm used to look in contrast to its appearance today. The photo below, taken a few years later in about 1922 shows Hugh's sister Ann in Girl Guide's uniform outside the farm. Several of the postcards in this collection had belonged to Ann.

Hugh and Ann's father at work on the farm hay cutting. A more tranquil scene than today's mechanical farming methods.

Hugh Harrison on the left, in about 1914, feeding the hens at Marsh Farm, and below, still farming in the 1950s.

Another postcard from Ann Harrison's collection shows her grandfather William Harrison (left) helping neighbour Henry Walton with his harvest.

Researching for this book has been a great joy, but with some puzzles. These three photographs are inscribed on the back, but I have found no information to substantiate what is written. The cottage is said to have been in Pope Lane, Whitestake, yet I can find nothing to verify this, nor find it anywhere in the catchment area. Similarly, the man with the gun may by Nathan Harrison and the man alongside the farm gate Thomas Harrison of Marsh Farm. This isn't Marsh Farm but these two chaps may be related to the Harrrison family who worked Marsh Farm for many years, though it must be remembered that unrelated families often had the same surname.